Delicious and Easy Fi Toast Recipes

Simple but Tasty French Toast Anyone Can Make

BY: Nancy Silverman

COPYRIGHT NOTICES

Table of Contents

Introduction

Do you ever think about making homemade breakfast? When you wake up, do you just feel like you do not have the time or energy to cook? Have you ever thought about making French toast, but it seemed too complicated?

In this book, you will learn how to make super easy French toast recipes – 32 of them. Some of them are casseroles you can prepare the night before, while others are meals you can make in 15-20 minutes. The recipes are easy to make, have simple ingredients, and can be scaled up or down depending on how many people you are cooking.

I wrote this recipe book because I believe French toast is delicious and super easy to make, but it can look more complicated. This makes people feel like they could never make these delicious breakfast dishes on their own. I do not want people to miss out on all the different flavor combinations you can create with French toast or only feel like they can eat this in a restaurant.

In this book, you will find 32 recipes. Each recipe is easy to read and use. It will have the following:

- A title
- A short description or reason why you will want to make this recipe
- How many servings each recipe has
- How long you will be cooking
- The ingredients
- The Instructions

I invite you to keep reading to see how easy it can be to make French toast at home for you or others. You will be surprised by the ease of this food, as well as all of the delicious flavor and texture combinations you can use. Onto chapter one!

Apple Cinnamon French Toast

French Toast is already a sweet and scrumptious breakfast but adding a little apple cinnamon flavor just puts it over the top! Is it healthy? Is it Dessert or a Meal? Does it really matter? It is delicious and tasty no matter what time of the day you eat this heavenly recipe!

Serves: 4

Cook Time: 20 Minutes

Ingredients:

- 2 large apples
- ½ cup of sugar
- ½ tsp of cinnamon
- 7 tbsp of butter, divided
- 3 ½ tbsp of water, divided
- 8 slices of breadcrumb4 eggs
- ½ cup of milk

Instructions:

Heat cinnamon, sugar, 3 tbsp of butter in a small saucepan over medium heat.

At the same time, cut apples into ¼ inch slices.

Add apples and water to the saucepan. Stir and reduce to simmer. It will thicken to a syrup-like consistency.

While the apple slices are cooking, whisk together milk, eggs, salt, and the remaining butter in a medium bowl.

Pour a ¼ of the butter mixture into a large enough pan to cook 4 pieces of bread at once. Heat the butter mixture to medium-high.

Individually, dip each piece of bread into the bowl until coated but not soaked through.

Transfer 4 pieces of bread to the pan—Cook for 1 ½ to 2 minutes per side.

Repeat steps 6 and 7 with 4 remaining pieces of bread.

Serve French Toast with apple and syrup mixture on top and between the slices.

Baked French Toast

Baked French toast can be prepared and cooked immediately, or you can prepare this casserole and put it in your fridge overnight to have little to no prep time the following morning. This is a great casserole for Sunday mornings, brunch, holidays, or just because French toast is always a good idea! This recipe is written for cooking it immediately, but do not preheat your oven until needed if you are preparing for the following day.

Serves: 8

Cook Time: 1 Hour

Ingredients:

- Cooking spray
- 1 loaf of French or Italian bread
- 2 cups of 1% or 2% milk
- ½ cup of heavy cream
- ½ cup of white sugar
- 1 cup of brown sugar, divided
- 2 tbsp of vanilla
- ½ cup of flour
- 1 ½ tsp of cinnamon
- ½ tsp of salt
- 8 oz of butter, cold, and cut into small pieces
- Fresh fruit for topping, if desired

Instructions:

Spray a 13 x 9 pan with cooking spray—Preheat oven to 350 degrees F.

Tear bread into small chunks and evenly distribute it in the cooking pan.

In a large bowl, whisk together milk, cream, eggs, white sugar, ½ cup of brown sugar, and vanilla until well combined. Pour over bread evenly. Cover and put it into the fridge until needed.

Prepare the topping – mix together the remaining brown sugar (½ cup, firmly packed), flour, cinnamon, and salt. Mix with fork. Add the butter pieces and mix them together with a pastry cutter until the mixture looks like small pebbles.

Pour a ¼ of the butter mixture into a large enough pan to cook 4 pieces of bread at once. Heat the butter mixture to medium-high.

If you are not making French toast now, store it in a small plastic bag in the fridge.

To prepare casserole – sprinkle topping onto casserole contents. Bake for 50 minutes if you want soft French toast; bake for 60 minutes if you want crispier French toast.

Serve individual pieces with butter and syrup. Add a fresh fruit topping if desired.

Berry Stuffed French Toast

If you love your berries, this is the French toast recipe for you. The recipe includes a berry syrup that uses blueberries, black raspberries and red raspberries, and deliciously sweet French toast. This is a great recipe when you can get fresh fruit. However, you can also use frozen fruit to enjoy this delightful French toast all year long!

Serves: 8

Cook Time: 30 Minutes

Ingredients:

- 1 cup of red raspberries
- ½ cup of blueberries
- ½ cup of black raspberries
- additional fruit for topping
- ¾ cup of light brown sugar, packed
- 3 tbsp of butter
- 3 tsp of cinnamon, divided
- 3 tsp of vanilla, divided
- ½ cup of sour cream
- 8 ounces of cream cheese, softened
- 16 slices of sourdough bread
- ½ cup of fruit preserves (berry flavor of choice)
- 6 eggs
- ¼ cup of half and half

Instructions:

Prepare your Syrup: combine fruit, butter, brown sugar, and 1 ½ tsp of cinnamon in a medium saucepan. Bring syrup ingredients to a boil. Reduce heat to simmer. Simmer uncovered for 4-6 minutes. Remove from heat and set aside.

In a medium-sized bowl, beat together sour cream and cream cheese—spread mixture on 8 slices of bread.

Combine fruit preserves and 1 tsp of vanilla. Spread this over the remaining 8 slices of bread. Make sandwiches by matching one cream cheese slice of bread with 1 preserves slice of bread—place bread, cream cheese side down.

In a shallow bowl such as a pie dish, combine half and half, eggs, and 1 ½ tsp of cinnamon. Dip both sides of sandwiches into this mixture. Dip to coat, not soak. Cook sandwiches on a hot skillet or griddle for 3-4 minutes per side.

Cut the French toast sandwiches diagonally. Serve with the berry syrup. Add additional fresh fruit as a topping if desired.

Baked Blueberry French Toast

Blueberry is the go-to ingredient for all tasty breakfast foods such as muffins, pancakes, waffles, and quick bread. This is no different with French toast. This will quickly become your favorite blueberry breakfast recipe ever.

Serves: 7

Cook Time: 1 Hour

Ingredients:

- 14 slices of bread
- 16 ounces of cream cheese, chilled
- 2 ½ cups of blueberries, rinsed and drained, divided
- 1 dozen eggs, lightly beaten
- 2 cups of 1% or 2% milk
- ¼ cup of honey
- 1 cup of white sugar
- 1 cup of water
- 2 tbsp of cornstarch
- 1 tbsp of butter

Instructions:

Spray a 13 x 9 pan with cooking spray—Preheat oven to 350 degrees F.

Tear half of the bread into small chunks and evenly distribute it in the cooking pan. Cut cream cheese into 1-inch cubes, sprinkle over bread pieces. Top with 1 ½ cups of blueberries and the remaining bread pieces.

Whisk together honey, milk, and eggs in a small bowl. Pour into the casserole dish evenly over the bread. Cover and put in the fridge for at least 60 minutes, but as long as overnight.

Remove casserole dish from the fridge for at least 30 minutes before cooking. Cover with foil and bake for 30 minutes at 350 degrees F. Remove foil and bake for another 20-25 minutes. To check for doneness, insert a knife into the center; it should come out clean.

After you remove the foil, you will prepare the blueberry syrup. Combine sugar, water, and cornstarch in a saucepan until all ingredients are smooth. At medium heat, bring to a boil. Stir until it thickens; this will take 3-4 minutes. Stir in remaining blueberries. And bring back to a boil. Lower to a simmer and cook for 9-11 minutes until blueberries burst. Remove from heat and stir in butter. Serve with the blueberry French toast.

Blueberry Pecan Topped French Toast

This recipe is ideal when you are looking for a more basic French toast base with a sweet and savory topping. The blueberries and pecans really bring this entire dish together.

Serves: 4

Cook Time: 30 Minutes

Ingredients:

- 8 slices of bread
- 2 eggs
- ½ cup of 2% milk
- ½ tsp of vanilla
- 2/3 tsp of cinnamon
- 1 cup of pecans
- dash of salt
- 1 ½ cup of blueberries, divided
- 1 cup of warm water
- 1 cup of white sugar
- 1 ½ tsp of lemon juice

Instructions:

Preheat oven to 325 degrees F.

Make the Blueberry Syrup – Mix together warm water, 1 cup of blueberries, white sugar, and lemon juice into a small saucepan. Heat over low heat until the sugar has dissolved; this will take 5-7 minutes. Turn up to medium and bring to a gentle boil until the syrup has thickened. This will take approximately 15 minutes. Remove from heat.

Line a cookie sheet pan with parchment paper and put pecans on the cookie sheet in a single layer—Cook for 8 minutes. Remove from oven.

Beat eggs well in a small bowl. Add vanilla, cinnamon, and milk. Beat well.

Dunk each piece of bread into a bowl. You want the bread coated, not soaked. Cook on a non-stick skillet or an electric griddle on medium-high heat for 2-3 minutes per side.

To Serve: put French toast on plates. Top with pecans, then blueberry syrup. Enjoy.

Bananas Foster French Toast

Banana fosters French toast is an indulgence, one that you should take part in as much as you can. It is French toast topped with sweet and sticky bananas in a delicious rum and brown sugar syrup. Although the taste is delicious, it is far easier to make than you would think!

Serves: 6

Cook Time: 30 Minutes

Ingredients:

- 12 slices of brioche bread
- 12 tbsp of butter, divided
- 4 eggs
- 1½ cups of whole milk
- 1 ½ tsp of vanilla
- 1 ½ tsp of cinnamon
- ½ cup of dark brown sugar, packed
- ¼ cup of maple syrup
- 1 tsp of rum extract
- ¼ – ½ cup of chopped pecans
- 2 large bananas, sliced

Instructions:

Preheat oven to 250 degrees F.

Whisk together eggs, brown sugar, whole milk, cinnamon, and vanilla in a medium bowl. This is the custard you will use to dip your bread in.

Melt 6 tbsp of butter on a griddle for frying. In small batches, dip bread in custard and let excess liquid drip off. Bread should be coated, not soaked. Cook on the griddle over medium heat for 2-3 minutes per side. Place on a baking rack in preheated oven to keep warm. Repeat with the remaining bread until it is all cooked and being kept warm in your oven.

Make your sauce – heat the remaining butter in a pan over medium-high heat—whisk in the maple syrup and brown sugar. Cook for 4-6 minutes until all the sugar is melted and the sauce has slightly thickened.

Add pecans to taste, mix to combine. Add sliced bananas and cook for 1-2 minutes. Remove from heat and add rum extract (for a more authentic taste, you could use ¼ cup of dark rum instead of extract). Return to heat and cook for an additional 4-5 minutes.

Serve by placing French toast on plates and spooning the syrup and bananas on top.

Banana Hazelnut French Toast

This French toast recipe will be great for breakfast, lunch, or dinner. The bananas add enough healthy food to justify a meal. Still, the hazelnut spread can even make this French toast recipe work as a delicious snack or dessert.

Serves: 4

Cook Time: 20 Minutes

Ingredients:

- 8 slices of bread
- 2 bananas, sliced
- ½ cup of chocolate hazelnut spread
- ½ cup of 2% or whole chocolate milk
- 4 eggs, beaten
- 1 ½ tsp of vanilla
- 1 tsp of cinnamon
- 4 tbsp of butter

Instructions:

Spread Nutella (or other chocolate hazelnut spread) on one side of each piece of bread. On 4 of those slices, arrange the banana slices on top of the Nutella. Make a sandwich by putting other bread with Nutella on top.

Whisk together eggs, vanilla extract, cinnamon, and chocolate milk in a medium bowl— dip sandwiches to coat each side, but not soak through.

On an electric griddle or in a large skillet, melt the butter over medium heat. Cook the French toast sandwiches for 4-5 minutes per side.

Baked Cranberry Apple French Toast

These flavors work well in the Autumn or during the holiday season. However, you do not need to wait to enjoy cranberry-apple French toast; this would be a lovely treat any time of the year.

Serves: 10

Cook Time: 40 Minutes

Ingredients:

- 1 loaf of bread, French or Italian works best, cut into thick slices
- 1 cup of brown sugar
- 8 tbsp (1 stick) of butter, melted
- 6 eggs
- 1 ½ cups of milk
- 1 ½ tbs vanilla
- 3 tsp cinnamon
- 3 apples, peeled, cored, and thinly sliced
- ½ cup of dried cranberries

Instructions:

Combine melted butter, brown sugar, and 1 teaspoon of cinnamon in a medium bowl. Add cranberries and apples, toss to coat. Spread fruit mixture at the baking dish bottom. Place bread slices on top evenly.

In a bowl, whisk together vanilla, 2 teaspoons of cinnamon, milk, and eggs until well blended. Pour the mixture on the bread evenly.

Cover and place the baking pan in the fridge for at least 4 hours, up to 24 hours.

Bake French toast casserole cover for 40 minutes.

Chocolate French Toast

Chocolate breakfast items like pancakes, French toast, or waffles are sometimes just what you need. This can be a weekend treat, a meal to get you through the day, or even a decadent dinner after a long day. It is delicious and easy to make.

Serves: 4

Cook Time: 30 Minutes

Ingredients:

- 8 slices of bread
- ¼ cup of hot water
- ¼ cup of cocoa powder
- 6 eggs
- ½ cup of heavy cream
- 1 cup of 2% milk
- ¼ cup of white sugar
- 1 ½ tsp of vanilla
- ½ tsp of salt
- 4 tbsp of butter
- 12 oz of milk chocolate morsels

Instructions:

Place cocoa powder in a small bowl and add the hot water to dissolve it. Stir until blended. Set aside.

In a shallow dish, whisk together the eggs, milk, cream, sugar, salt, and vanilla. Once well combined, add cocoa mixture and stir again.

melt butter on a griddle or large skillet at medium-high heat. Dip on a slice of bread to coat. Put in skillet. Add chocolate morsels on top. Dip another slice of bread. Place on top to form a sandwich. Repeat with remaining bread and chocolate morsels.

Cook for 3-4 minutes per side to melt chocolate morsels.

Slow Cooker Chocolate Milk French Toast

Want a sweet and delightful French toast meal but would instead use your slow cooker? This is a deliciously chocolatey French toast dish made with chocolate milk. What more could you ask for?

Serves: 6

Cook Time: 2 hours 45 Minutes

Ingredients:

- 16 ounces of bread, cut into 1-inch cubes
- 2 tbsp of brown sugar
- 1 ½ tsp of cinnamon
- ½ tsp of salt
- 6 eggs
- 2 cups of chocolate milk
- ¾ cup of heavy cream
- 1 tbsp of buttermilk
- 4 oz of chocolate chips

Instructions:

Place bread cubes on a cookie sheet and cook for 15 minutes in an oven preheated to 325 degrees F.

In a large bowl, combine cinnamon, brown sugar, salt, and eggs. In a small bowl, combine chocolate milk and heavy cream. Add milk and cream mixture to the first bowl and whisk until smooth.

Grease inside of the slow cooker. Add about half of the bread cubes and top with ¼ of the chocolate chips. Pour in the rest of the bread, then the chocolate milk mixture on top. Chill in the fridge for 2 hours.

Take slow cooker insert out of the fridge and warm back up to room temperature for 30 minutes.

Cook in your slow cooker on high for 2 ½ hours. Sprinkle remaining chocolate chips on top—Cook for an additional 15 minutes.

Coconut French Toast

Coconut French toast is an excellent choice for a basic recipe with just a little extra texture and flavor.

Serves: 4

Cook Time: 20 Minutes

Ingredients:

- 8 slices of bread
- ½ cup of milk
- ½ cup of coconut milk
- ¼ cup of white sugar
- 1 ½ tsp of vanilla
- ½ tsp of cinnamon
- 6 eggs
- 2 cups of shredded coconut
- 3 tbsp of butter

Instructions:

Beat together eggs, milk, coconut milk, sugar, vanilla, and cinnamon in a shallow dish. In another shallow dish, pour in the coconut.

Heat an electric skillet or a large skillet over medium-high heat with butter, melt it.

Dip the bread one slice at a time in the milk and egg mixture. Dip until well coated but not soaked. Then dip both sides into coconut flakes.

Cook on griddle or skillet for 2-3 minutes per side, careful not to burn due to the sugar in the coconut.

Churro French Toast

Churros French toast is a great treat – French toast with cinnamon sugar and a delicious cream cheese topping. This can be served for a weekend breakfast or even as a dessert.

Serves: 4

Cook Time: 20 Minutes

Ingredients:

Cinnamon Sugar:

- ½ cup of white sugar
- 3 tsp of cinnamon
- 1/3 cup of brown sugar

Cream Cheese Frosting:

- 4 tbsp of cream cheese, softened
- ½ cup of powdered sugar
- 2 tbsp of milk

French Toast:

- 8 slices of bread
- 4 eggs
- 2 cups of milk
- ¼ cup of brown sugar
- 1 ½ tsp of cinnamon
- 1 tsp of vanilla
- 4 tbsp of butter

Instructions:

Make the Cinnamon Sugar-combine cinnamon sugar ingredients in a shallow dish. Set aside.

Whisk together eggs, milk, brown sugar, cinnamon, and vanilla in a large bowl.

Dip the bread one slice at a time in the milk and egg mixture.

Heat up griddle or skillet to medium heat with the 4 tbsp of butter, until melted. Cook on griddle or skillet for 2-3 minutes per side.

Remove from skillet and toss into cinnamon sugar. Place on wire rack.

Make the icing-combine icing ingredients in a small bowl. Stir until smooth.

Drizzle each of the slices with icing.

Baked Cinnamon Roll French Toast

Although French toast is a delicious treat all on its own – why not combine a French toast bake with the sweetness of cinnamon rolls? Enjoy this decadent and scrumptious breakfast today!

Serves: 4

Cook Time: 20 Minutes

Ingredients:

- 1 (12 oz) can of cinnamon rolls
- Cooking spray
- 4 eggs
- ¼ cup of whole milk
- 1 ½ tsp of vanilla
- 1 ½ tsp of cinnamon

Instructions:

preheat oven to 375 degrees F. Spray 13-9 baking dish with cooking spray.

Cut each cinnamon roll into 6-8 pieces. Place the cinnamon roll pieces in the bottom of the baking dish.

In a large bowl, mix eggs, milk, vanilla, and cinnamon—pour over rolls.

Bake the casserole in a preheated oven for 25-30 minutes. Squeeze the frosting packet, which can with cinnamon rolls on top.

Angel Food French Toast

Here is a light and fluffy version of French toast using a store-bought or premade angel food cake. Topped with berries and whipped cream, and this is the perfect breakfast treat.

Serves: 6

Cook Time: 20 Minutes

Ingredients:

- 1 prepared angel food cake, cut into 12 pieces
- 4 eggs
- 1 cup of milk
- 2 tsp of vanilla
- ½ tsp of cinnamon
- ¼ tsp of salt
- 4 tbsp of butter
- Toppings – whipped cream, sliced strawberries, blueberries, syrup, powdered sugar

Instructions:

Slice angel food cake and set aside.

In a large bowl, mix together the eggs, milk, vanilla, salt, and cinnamon.

Melt butter on a griddle heated to medium. Dip the cake slices into the milk and egg mixture, coating but not soaking the bread. Fry for 2-3 minutes per side.

Serve with desired toppings, including whipped cream, fresh berries, powdered sugar, or syrup.

Eggnog French Toast

Although you can easily make this French toast recipe anytime, it is great to celebrate the holidays or serve at holiday gatherings.

Serves: 6

Cook Time: 20 Minutes

Ingredients:

- 12 slices of bread
- 2 cups of eggnog
- 2 tsp of cinnamon
- 1 tsp of vanilla
- 1 tsp of pumpkin pie spice
- 3 eggs
- 3 tbsp of butter

Instructions:

In a large bowl, mix together the eggs, eggnog, cinnamon, vanilla, and pumpkin pie spice.

Dunk the bread in the egg/milk mixture. You want to coat but not soak evenly.

Melt butter on a griddle at medium-high heat. Cook bread 2-3 minutes per side.

Easy French Toast

Sometimes you just want a basic and easy French toast recipe. Here is a no-frills French toast you can have on the table in 10 minutes.

Serves: 6

Cook Time: 20 Minutes

Ingredients:

- 12 slices of bread
- ½ cup of milk
- 2 eggs
- 2 tsp of vanilla
- 1 tsp of cinnamon

Instructions:

In a large bowl, mix together the eggs, milk, cinnamon, and vanilla.

Dunk the bread in the egg/milk mixture. You want to coat but not soak evenly.

Melt butter on a griddle at medium-high heat. Cook bread 2-3 minutes per side.

Suppose you want something extra in this recipe. In that case, you can do so with different toppings, including flavored syrup, powdered sugar, fresh fruit, or even whipped cream.

Gingerbread French Toast

Gingerbread is another excellent flavor we associate with the holiday season. You can either serve this during the holidays or indulge in this sweet breakfast treat all year long!

Serves: 4

Cook Time: 20 Minutes

Ingredients:

- 8 slices of bread
- 1 cup of milk
- 4 eggs
- 2 tbsp of sugar
- 1 1/3 tbsp of rum extract
- 1 ½ tsp of salt
- 1 tsp of cinnamon
- ¾ tsp of nutmeg
- ¼ tsp of cloves
- ¼ tsp of ginger
- 4 tbsp of butter

Instructions:

Mix together all the ingredients except the butter and bread until well combined in a medium to a large bowl.

Dunk the bread in the egg/milk mixture. You want to coat but not soak evenly.

Melt butter on a griddle at medium-high heat. Cook bread 2-3 minutes per side.

Hot Chocolate French Toast

Hot chocolate is a flavor that brings us back to our childhood and makes us feel warm, cozy and comforted. This recipe will allow you to include that taste in a sweet and delicious breakfast French toast recipe.

Serves: 4

Cook Time: 20 Minutes

Ingredients:

- 8 slices of cinnamon bread
- 1 cup of milk
- 4 eggs
- ¼ cup of hot cocoa mix
- 1 ½ tsp of vanilla
- 1 tsp of cinnamon
- 8 ounces of milk chocolate morsels
- 4 tbsp of butter
- Chocolate syrup and whipped cream for topping

Instructions:

Mix together the eggs, milk, hot cocoa mix, vanilla, and cinnamon in a medium to large bowl.

Dunk the bread in the egg/milk mixture. You want to evenly coat but not soak.

Melt butter on a griddle at medium-high heat. Place 4 slices of bread on the griddle. Split the chocolate morsels between these 4 slices. Cook for 3-4 minutes until melted. Create 4 French toast sandwiches by adding another slice of bread on top of the first. Flip your French toast sandwich and cook for an additional 2-3 minutes.

Serve topped with a dollop of whipped cream and a drizzle of chocolate syrup on top.

Orange Almond French Toast Bake

This is an orange French toast bake with an almond crumble topping. It is like eating a cross between a flavored French toast casserole and a deliciously textured coffee cake.

Serves: 8

Cook Time: 40 Minutes

Ingredients:

- 1 loaf of French bread
- 4 eggs
- 1 ½ cups of milk
- 3 tbsp of sugar
- 2 tsp of vanilla
- ½ tsp of cinnamon
- 3 tbsp of orange extract
- Cooking spray
- 3 tbsp of butter
- ½ cup of brown sugar
- ½ cup of oats
- ½ cup of almonds, silvered

Instructions:

Spray 13x9 pan with cooking spray. Set aside.

Slice your loaf of French bread into ¾ inch to 1-inch slices—place in cooking dish.

In a small bowl, combine milk, eggs, sugar, cinnamon, vanilla, and orange extract. Pour it over French bread.

Combine brown sugar, butter, oats, and almonds in a medium to a bowl. Pour over the casserole dish evenly. Cover your casserole dish with foil and refrigerator for 4 hours or up to overnight.

Preheat your oven (350 degrees F). Place the French toast casserole dish into the preheated oven and bake uncovered for 40-45 minutes.

Overnight French Toast Bake

This is a slightly healthier French toast bake using wheat bread and fresh berries! If you are not sure you want to indulge in such a sweet breakfast option as French toast, this will allow you to get some more grains and fruit into the recipe.

Serves: 8

Cook Time: 35 Minutes

Ingredients:

- 1 loaf of white wheat bread
- 4 eggs
- 1 ½ cups of 1% milk
- 2 tbsp of sugar
- 2 tsp of vanilla
- ½ tsp of cinnamon
- ¼ tsp of salt
- ¼ cup of maple syrup
- Topping: Greek yogurt and fresh berries

Instructions:

Spray 13x9 pan with cooking spray. Set aside.

Slice your loaf of wheat bread into ¾ inch to 1-inch slices—place in cooking dish.

In a small bowl, combine eggs, milk, sugar, vanilla, cinnamon, salt, and maple syrup. Pour over wheat bread.

Cover and refrigerator for at least 4 hours, up to overnight.

When you are ready to bake, preheat the oven to 375 degrees F. Place casserole dish into the preheated oven and bake covered for 20 minutes. Uncover and bake for an additional 15 minutes.

Serve topped with Greek yogurt and fresh berries.

Orange French Toast

If orange is one of your favorite flavors and aromas, you will love this recipe. This easy French toast recipe will quickly become one of your favorites. It is easy to make, does not have too many ingredients, and will be on your breakfast table in no time.

Serves: 4

Cook Time: 15 Minutes

Ingredients:

- 8 slices of bread
- 3 tbsp of butter
- ½ tsp of cinnamon
- 1 tsp of vanilla
- ¼ tsp of salt
- 4 eggs
- ¾ cup of orange juice
- 1 tbsp of orange extract
- 2 tbsp of honey

Instructions:

In a small bowl, combine eggs, orange juice, vanilla, cinnamon, salt, orange extract, and honey.

Melt butter on the electric griddle at medium heat.

Dip bread in egg/orange juice mixture. Cook on heated up griddle for 3-4 minutes per side.

Maple Bacon French Toast

This recipe is for when you are looking for a hearty breakfast with just a touch of protein to start your day. You can either precook the bacon or use microwave bacon strips to make this recipe takes no time.

Serves: 4

Cook Time: 15 Minutes

Ingredients:

- 8 slices of bread
- 3 tbsp of butter
- ½ tsp of cinnamon
- 1 tsp of vanilla
- ¼ tsp of salt
- 4 eggs
- 1 cup of milk
- 1/3 cup of maple syrup
- 8 slices of bacon, cooked and crumbled

Instructions:

In a small bowl, combine eggs, milk, vanilla, cinnamon, salt, and maple syrup. Stir to combine.

Melt butter on the electric griddle at medium heat.

Dip bread in egg/milk mixture. Cook on heated up griddle for 3-4 minutes per side.

Serve on plates with crumbled bacon on top of each slice and between slices.

Pumpkin French Toast

There is no other flavor that captures the essence of the fall better than pumpkin. So, enjoy this quick but delicious recipe any time you are in the mood for the earthy flavors of pumpkin or pumpkin spice.

Serves: 4

Cook Time: 15 Minutes

Ingredients:

- 8 slices of bread
- 3 tbsp of butter
- ½ tsp of cinnamon
- ¼ tsp of cloves
- ¼ tsp of nutmeg
- 1/8 tsp of ginger
- ½ cup of pumpkin puree
- 1 tsp of vanilla
- ¼ tsp of salt
- 4 eggs
- 1 cup of milk
- Topping – whipped cream and pumpkin pie spice

Instructions:

In a small bowl, combine everything but the bread and butter.

Melt butter on the electric griddle at medium heat.

Dip bread in egg/milk mixture. Cook on heated up griddle for 3-4 minutes per side.

Serve on plates with a dollop of whipped cream sprinkled with pumpkin pie spice.

Peanut Butter and Jelly or Jam French Toast

Peanut butter and jelly/jam is a favorite lunchtime sandwich, but it tastes even better in the morning. These peanut butter and jelly French toast sandwiches are delicious and super easy to make!

Serves: 4

Cook Time: 15 Minutes

Ingredients:

- 8 slices of bread
- 3 tbsp of butter
- ½ tsp of cinnamon
- 1 tsp of vanilla
- ¼ tsp of salt
- 4 eggs
- 1 cup of milk
- ½ cup of peanut butter
- 4-6 tablespoons of jam or jelly
- Topping – syrup or powdered sugar, fresh berries

Instructions:

In a small bowl, combine milk, eggs, vanilla, cinnamon, and salt.

Melt butter on the electric griddle at medium heat.

Divide your bread into 2 equal piles. Spread jam or jelly on half of them and peanut butter on the remaining pieces. Combine to make a peanut butter and jam/jelly sandwich.

Dip sandwiches in egg/milk mixture. Cook on heated up griddle for 3-4 minutes per side.

Serve on plates with desired toppings, including powdered sugar or syrup. Matching fresh fruit would do especially well. For example, if you used raspberry jam on the sandwiches, serve with fresh raspberries.

Pear Stuffed French Toast

Are you looking for a fresh fruit French toast recipe? Try this pear stuffed French toast recipe today. It is delicious and much easier to make than you would think!

Serves: 4

Cook Time: 15 Minutes

Ingredients:

- 8 slices of bread
- 5 tbsp of butter, melted
- ½ tsp of cinnamon
- 1 tsp of vanilla
- ¼ tsp of salt
- 4 eggs
- 1 cup of milk
- 2 pears, peeled and chopped – chilled in the fridge
- Cooking spray

Instructions:

Mix together chopped pears and melted butter. Mash them together to create a paste or spread.

In a small bowl, combine milk, eggs, vanilla, cinnamon, and salt.

Spray an electric griddle with cooking spray at medium heat.

On four slices of bread, divide the pear spread between them. Then, place the other 4 slices on top to create pear stuffed sandwiches.

Dip sandwiches in egg/milk mixture. Cook on heated griddle for 3-4 minutes per side.

Pistachio Crusted French Toast

Are you a fan of pistachio nuts? Then, try this pistachio-crusted baked French toast recipe. The nuts bring extra flavor as well as more texture to this breakfast casserole.

Serves: 8

Cook Time: 50 Minutes

Ingredients:

- 1 loaf of French bread, sliced into 3/4-inch to 1-inch pieces
- 1 ¼ cups of chopped white chocolate, divided
- 1 ½ cups of heavy cream
- ½ cup of milk
- 8 oz of cream cheese, softened
- 8 eggs
- ¼ cup of honey plus 3 tbsp
- 2 tsp almond extract
- 1 tsp of vanilla
- 2 tsp of cinnamon, divided
- 8 oz of butter, melted
- ½ cup of brown sugar
- ¾ cup of pistachios, finely chopped

Instructions:

Spray the bottom of a baking dish with cooking spray. Cover the bottom with sliced French bread.

In a large, microwave-safe bowl, combine heavy cream and 1 cup of chopped white chocolate. Heat to melt chocolate, about 4-5 minutes.

In another bowl, beat together cream cheese and milk until smooth. Pour into white chocolate and cream bowl.

Whisk in eggs, ¼ cup of honey, almond extract, vanilla, and 1 tsp of cinnamon. Pour it over French bread slices.

Cover and refrigerate for at least 1 hour, but up to 24 hours.

preheat oven to 350 degrees F. Remove French toast casserole from the fridge.

Prepare topping. In a small bowl, combine brown sugar, melted butter, 3 tbsp of honey, and 1 tsp of cinnamon. Stir in ¼ cup of white chocolate. Sprinkle over French bread casserole.

Bake covered for 40 minutes. Uncover and bake for an additional 12-15 minutes.

Peanut Butter Stuffed French Toast

If you are a peanut butter lover, you will just adore these peanut butter stuffed French toast sandwiches. You can top them with sliced bananas and drizzle honey on top for a little extra taste and nod to these sandwiches. Delicious.

Serves: 4

Cook Time: 20 Minutes

Ingredients:

- 8 slices of bread
- ½ cup of creamy or chunky peanut butter
- 1 cup of milk
- 4 eggs
- 1 tsp vanilla
- 1 tsp cinnamon
- ¼ tsp of salt
- Topping – honey and 2 sliced bananas

Instructions:

In a small bowl, combine milk, eggs, vanilla, cinnamon, and salt.

Melt butter on the electric griddle at medium heat.

Spread peanut butter on all the bread slices and then make 4 sandwiches.

Dip sandwiches in egg/milk mixture. Cook on heated griddle for 3-4 minutes per side.

Serve on plates with desired toppings, including powdered sugar or syrup. You can also slice 1-2 bananas and top each stuffed peanut butter French toast sandwich with sliced bananas and then drizzle honey on top.

Strawberry Lemon French Toast

This is a sweet and tangy French toast recipe for you to enjoy. Lemon French toast, which is topped with sweet strawberries, will make any morning exceptional.

Serves: 4

Cook Time: 30 Minutes

Ingredients:

- 8 slices of bread, cubed
- 2 cups of macerated strawberries
- 4 eggs
- 1 cup of milk
- 2 tbsp of maple syrup
- 1 tbsp of lemon juice
- 1 lemon, zested
- 2 tsp vanilla
- 3 tsp of cinnamon, divided
- ½ cup of flour
- ¼ cup of light brown sugar, packed
- ¼ cup of butter, cold and cubed
- Cooking spray

Instructions:

Spray cooking spray into a 13x9 casserole dish. Pour bread cubes into the dish to cover the bottom.

Combine milk, eggs, maple syrup, lemon juice, lemon zest, vanilla, and 1 tsp of cinnamon. Pour on top of the bread.

Make Crumb Topping: In a small bowl, combine flour, brown sugar, butter, and 2 tbsp of cinnamon. Work into it resembles coarse crumbs. Evenly top the casserole with this mixture.

Bake in an oven preheated to 350 degrees F. Cook for 25-30 minutes.

Serve warm topped with macerated strawberries.

NOTE: To macerate strawberries: Put strawberry slices in a medium-sized bowl. Add sugar (1-2 tbsp per cup of strawberries) Either let sit at room temperature for 30 minutes or place in the fridge for longer. The sugar will pull the sweetness out and make them taste better and create a sweet sugar and strawberry sauce.

Strawberry Rhubarb French Toast Bake

Strawberry Rhubarb is a classic flavor combination that goes together splendidly. Try this recipe this week – make the casserole ahead of time the day before, and then just wake up and pop it in the oven for this deliciously fruity breakfast treat.

Serves: 8

Cook Time: 50 Minutes

Ingredients:

- 1 loaf of sourdough bread, cubed
- ½ cup of milk
- 10 eggs
- ¾ cup of maple syrup
- 2 tsp of cinnamon, divided
- 1 ½ tsp of vanilla
- 2 cups of strawberries, sliced
- ½ cup of rhubarb, chopped
- ½ cup of flour
- ½ cup of sugar
- 8 ounces of butter, cold and cubed

Instructions:

Spray cooking spray into a 13x9 casserole dish. Pour bread cubes into the dish to cover the bottom.

Combine milk, eggs, maple syrup,1 tsp of cinnamon, and vanilla. Pour on top of the bread. Sprinkle rhubarb and strawberries equally on top.

Cover and refrigerate overnight.

Make Crumb Topping. In a small bowl, combine flour, sugar, butter, and 1 tbsp of cinnamon. Work into it resembles coarse crumbs. Evenly top the casserole with this mixture.

Bake in an oven preheated to 350 degrees F. Cook for 45-50 minutes.

Serve warm.

Strawberry Cream Cheese French Toast Bake

Strawberry Cream cheese is also a popular flavor; many people use strawberry cream cheese on their morning bagels. If it is good enough for bagels, why not also use this flavor in your French toast? This recipe is for a delicious French toast bake, something you can prepare the night before, allowing breakfast time to be a breeze.

Serves: 8

Cook Time: 60 Minutes

Ingredients:

- 1 lb. of brioche
- 8 oz of cream cheese, cubed, cubed
- 16 oz of strawberries, sliced and divided
- 2 cups of milk
- 10 eggs
- 1/3 cup of maple syrup
- 1 tsp of cinnamon
- 1 ½ tsp of vanilla

Instructions:

Spray cooking spray into a 13x9 casserole dish. Pour half of the bread cubes into the dish to cover the bottom. Now put in half of the strawberries and all of the cream cheese. Top with the remaining bread cubes.

Combine milk, eggs, maple syrup, cinnamon, and vanilla. Pour on top of the bread.

Cover and refrigerate for at least 1 hour, but up to overnight.

Preheat oven to 350 degrees F.

Bake in preheated oven for 55-60 minutes.

Serve warm with remaining strawberries and powdered sugar.

Sausage Stuffed French Toast

Adding sausage to your French toast will allow you to have a much more filling and savory breakfast. These thick slices of French toast will be filling and delicious, a fabulous way to start any day.

Serves: 4

Cook Time: 20 Minutes

Ingredients:

- Italian bread, sliced into 1 ½ to 2-inch slices (8 slices total)
- 8 sausage patties, fully cooked
- shredded sharp cheddar cheese, about 4 ounces
- 4 eggs
- 1 cup of milk
- 1 tsp of vanilla
- 1 tsp of cinnamon
- 4 tbsp of butter
- Syrup for serving

Instructions:

Cook sausage and set aside to cool slightly.

Combine milk, eggs, cinnamon, and vanilla.

Cut a pocket into each slice of bread and gently insert 1 fully cooked sausage patty and about ½ ounce of shredded cheese.

Dunk each slice of bread into milk/egg mixture to coat, not soak.

Warm up a griddle and melt 4 tbsp of butter. Fry the French toast on medium heat for 3-4 minutes per side.

Serve with syrup.

Salted Caramel French Toast

Sweet and Salty are two of the most critical flavors in any meal. Try this salted caramel French toast recipe today to experience them firsthand in an absolutely delicious way!

Serves: 4

Cook Time: 20 Minutes

Ingredients:

- 8 slices of bread
- 4 eggs
- 1 cup of milk
- 1 tsp of vanilla
- 1 tsp of cinnamon
- ¼ cup of sugar
- 1 jar of salted caramel sauce
- 4 tbsp of butter
- Syrup for serving
- Powdered sugar

Instructions:

Combine milk, eggs, cinnamon, sugar, and vanilla.

Dunk each slice of bread into milk/egg mixture to coat, not soak.

Warm up a griddle and melt 4 tbsp of butter. Fry the French toast on medium heat for 3-4 minutes per side.

Serve with powdered sugar, syrup, and salted caramel sauce for dipping.

Conclusion

There you have it – 32 delicious and easy French toast recipes. Now you can stop waiting until you go out for breakfast to enjoy this delicious food. You can make it as much or as little as you want. Also, please remember, French toast is not limited to breakfast. Breakfast meals are a great dinner option. Many of the recipes in this book would also work as a fun and modern dessert!

I hope you have learned some recipes that you cannot wait to try!

So, what should you do next?

Go back through this book and choose a few recipes you want to try this week. Start with a few simple ones and a few you just cannot wait to eat. This will motivate you to start cooking when you see how easy the recipes are.

Good luck and enjoy!

About the Author

Nancy Silverman is an accomplished chef from Essex, Vermont. Armed with her degree in Nutrition and Food Sciences from the University of Vermont, Nancy has excelled at creating e-books that contain healthy and delicious meals that anyone can make and everyone can enjoy. She improved her cooking skills at the New England Culinary Institute in Montpelier Vermont and she has been working at perfecting her culinary style since graduation. She claims that her life's work is always a work in progress and she only hopes to be an inspiration to aspiring chefs everywhere.

Her greatest joy is cooking in her modern kitchen with her family and creating inspiring and delicious meals. She often says that she has perfected her signature dishes based on her family's critique of each and every one.

Nancy has her own catering company and has also been fortunate enough to be head chef at some of Vermont's most exclusive restaurants. When a friend suggested she share some of her outstanding signature dishes, she decided to add cookbook author to her repertoire of personal achievements. Being a technological savvy woman, she felt the e-book realm would be a better fit and soon she had her first cookbook available online. As of today, Nancy has sold over 1,000 e-books and has shared her culinary experiences and brilliant recipes with people from all over the world! She plans on expanding into self-help books and dietary cookbooks, so stayed tuned!

Author's Afterthoughts

Thank you for making the decision to invest in one of my cookbooks! I cherish all my readers and hope you find joy in preparing these meals as I have.

There are so many books available and I am truly grateful that you decided to buy this one and follow it from beginning to end.

I love hearing from my readers on what they thought of this book and any value they received from reading it. As a personal favor, I would appreciate any feedback you can give in the form of a review on Amazon and please be honest! This kind of support will help others make an informed choice on and will help me tremendously in producing the best quality books possible.

My most heartfelt thanks,

Nancy Silverman

If you're interested in more of my books, be sure to follow my author page on Amazon (can be found on the link Bellow) or scan the QR-Code.

https://www.amazon.com/author/nancy-silverman

Printed in Great Britain
by Amazon

27335701R10051